Duck, Duck, Goose!

Written by Kirsten Hall

Illustrated by Laura Rader

My First
READER

children's press®

A Division of Scholastic Inc.

New York Toronto London Auckland Sydney
Mexico City New Delhi Hong Kong
Danbury, Connecticut

Library of Congress Cataloging-in-Publication Data

Hall, Kirsten.
  Duck, duck, goose! / written by Kirsten Hall ; illustrated by Laura
Rader.– [1st American ed.].
      p. cm. – (My first reader)
  Summary: When a boy plays the game "Duck, duck goose," his imagination
enables him to fly, moving faster than anyone else.
  ISBN 0-516-22925-7 (lib. bdg.)   0-516-24627-5 (pbk.)
  [1. Play–Fiction. 2. Imagination–Fiction.] I. Rader, Laura, ill. II.
Title. III. Series.
  PZ7.H1457Du 2003
  [E]–dc21
                                    2003003620

CHILDREN'S PRESS and associated logos are trademarks and or registered trademarks of Scholastic Library Publishing.
SCHOLASTIC and associated logos are trademarks and or registered trademarks of Scholastic Inc.

1 2 3 4 5 6 7 8 9 10 R 12 11 10 09 08 07 06 05 04 03

Note to Parents and Teachers

Once a reader can recognize and identify the 48 words
used to tell this story, he or she will be able to read successfully
the entire book. These 48 words are repeated throughout the story,
so that young readers will be able to easily recognize
the words and understand their meaning.

The 48 words used in this book are:

a	fast	it	run
again	faster	last	so
all	fly	let's	some
and	fox	like	the
back	fun	luck	this
be	goose	made	try
best	high	me	you
by	hooray	on	your
chase	I	pass	you're
come	I'll	past	wind
day	I'm	play	with
duck	is	rest	won't

Duck,

duck,

5

duck,

duck,

goose!

You're goose!

I'm on the run!

Run faster, faster, this is fun.

Come chase me, chase me

past the rest.

Come chase me, chase me.

Try your best.

I'm like a fox.

I run so fast.

I'm like a fox.

I fly so high.

I made it back.

Hooray! Hooray!

Let's play again.
Let's play all day!

Let's play again,
and with some luck,

I won't be goose.

I'll be a duck!

ABOUT THE AUTHOR

Kirsten Hall has lived most of her life in New York City. While she was still in high school, she published her first book for children, *Bunny, Bunny*. Since then, she has written and published more than sixty children's books. A former early education teacher, Kirsten currently works as a children's book editor.

ABOUT THE ILLUSTRATOR

Laura Rader was born in New Jersey and raised in Connecticut. She studied fine arts and graphic design at Pratt Institute in Brooklyn, New York, and has illustrated numerous books for children. Rader is now writing as well as illustrating. She currently lives in Los Angeles, California.